The Jellybean Band

written and illust

Flip-Flap, Sugar Snap!

by Susan James Frye

illustrated by Carol Koeller

Flip-flap, sugar snap,
Froggy in the peas,
Little Lena leaps along
As pretty as you please.

Flip to the east,
Flap to the west,
Flip-flap, Mama,
The way you like the best!

Boogie-woogie, waddle,
A-dip, dive, quack,
Sammy duck is hiding,
But he's coming right back.

Boogie to the east,
Woogie to the west,
Boogie-woogie, Daddy,
The way you like the best!

Float, teeter, fly,
Flit and glitter by,
Beau and Bitsy Butterfly
Flutter in the sky.

Float to the east,
Teeter to the west,
Float and teeter, Opa,
The way you like the best!

Whinny-shimmy, canter,
A-gallop, a-gallop, a-trot,
Stella Pony rides the trail
In every gear she's got.

Whinny to the east,
Shimmy to the west,
Whinny-shimmy, Auntie,
The way you like the best!

Sulla Lulla hula,
Down in the ocean deep,
Barcarollo Octopus
Has danced himself to sleep.

Sulla to the east,
Lulla to the west,
Sulla Lulla, bye-bye now—
I think you know the rest.

Where's My Home? illustrated by Mike Wohnoutka

All of these animals in the park need your help to get to their homes.
Follow the paths to find out where each one lives.